ROMAN JAKOBSON
AND STEPHEN RUDY

YEATS' "SORROW OF LOVE" THROUGH THE YEARS

LISSE

THE PETER DE RIDDER PRESS

1977

© 1977 by Roman Jakobson and Stephen Rudy

ISBN 90 316 0124 1

Photoset in Malta by Interprint (Malta) Ltd.

Printed in Holland by Intercontinental Graphics Dordrecht.

Why, what could she have done being what she is?
Was there another Troy for her to burn?

— "No Second Troy", 1910

CONTENTS

1. Introduction 7

2. Text and Variants 8

3. Composition 11

4. Grammar 14

5. -*ING*-Forms 15

6. Nouns 16

7. Prenominal Attributes 19

8. Postpositive Attributes 21

9. Pronouns 22

10. Adverbs 24

11. Articles 25

12. Connectives 27

13. Finite Verbs 29

14. Coordination and Subordination of Clauses 31

15. Predication 33

16. Sounds 35

17. Verse Pattern 39

18. Constructive Principles 42

19. Semantic Correspondences 48

References 54

1

INTRODUCTION

1.0   Paul Valéry, both a poet and an inquisitive theoretician of poetry as an 'art of language', recalls the story of the painter Degas, who loved to write poems, yet once complained to Mallarmé that he felt unable to achieve what he wanted in poetry despite being 'full of ideas'. Mallarmé's apt reply was: "Ce n'est point avec des idées, mon cher Degas, que l'on fait des vers. C'est avec des mots." (p. 141). In Valéry's view Mallarmé was right, for the essence of poetry lies precisely in the poetic transformation of verbal material and in the coupling of its phonetic and semantic aspects (cf. *ibid.*, p. 319).

1.1   William Butler Yeats, in a paper written in 1898 in favor of "art that is not mere story-telling", defended the notion that "pattern and rhythm are the road to open symbolism". According to Yeats, "the arts have already become full of pattern and rhythm. Subject pictures no longer interest us***". In this context he refers precisely to Degas, in Yeats' opinion an artist whose excessive and obstinate desire to 'picture' life — "and life at its most vivid and vigorous" — had harmed his work (*Memoirs*, p. 283f.). The poet's emphasis on pattern reminds one of Benjamin Lee Whorf, the penetrating linguist who realized that "the 'patternment' aspect of language always overrides and controls the 'lexation' or name-giving aspect" (1941:XXX), and an inquiry into the role of "pattern" in Yeats' own poetry becomes particularly attractive, especially when one is confronted with his constant and careful modifications of his own works.

TEXT AND VARIANTS

2.0 As early as 1899 Yeats stated that he "revised, and, to a great extent, re-wrote*** certain lyrics" (*Var.*, 846). His epigraph to *Collected Works in Verse and Prose* (Stratford-on-Avon, 1908) reads:

> The friends that have it I do wrong
> When ever I remake a song,
> Should know what issue is at stake:
> It is myself that I remake. (*Var.*, 778)

And in January, 1927 he mentions "new revisions on which my heart is greatly set" and adds, characteristically, "one is always cutting out the dead wood" (*Var.*, 848). For the 1925 edition of his *Early Poems and Prose* he "altered considerably" several of his poems, among them "The Sorrow of Love", "till they are altogether new poems. Whatever changes I have made are but an attempt to express better what I thought and felt when I was a very young man." (*Var.*, 842).

2.1 "The Sorrow of Love", which we will henceforth refer to as *SL*, is preserved in the poet's manuscript of October 1891 (*SL 1891*), then in two variants of 1892 differing slightly from each other, one published in the volume *The Countess Kathleen and Various Legends and Lyrics* (*SL 1892*) and the other in the weekly *The Independent* of October 20, 1892 (*SL 1892 Ind*). Later single changes appeared in Yeats' *Poems* (1895) and in their revised edition (1899). The radically reshaped text appeared first in Yeats' *Early Poems and Stories* (*SL 1925*), the notes to which, expressly mentioning *SL*, were quoted above. For an exhaustive survey of the text's history see *Var.* (119–120), G. Monteiro (1966:367–8), and R. Ellmann (1954:122 and 317 note).

2.2 The poet's "Sorrow of Love", which may be traced in its textual changes through over three decades, proved to be fruitful material for investigation. The comparative reproduction of *SL 1925* and the first version included in one of Yeats' volumes, *SL 1892*, with all other relevant textual variants, follows:

The Sorrow of Love
(Final version, 1925)

I
,The brawling of a sparrow in the eaves,
,The brilliant moon and all the milky sky,
,And all that famous harmony of leaves,
,Had blotted out man's image and his cry.

II
,A girl arose that had red mournful lips
,And seemed the greatness of the world in tears,
,Doomed like Odysseus and the labouring ships
,And proud as Priam murdered with his peers;

III
,Arose, and on the instant clamorous eaves,
,A climbing moon upon an empty sky,
,And all that lamentation of the leaves,
,Could but compose man's image and his cry.

The Sorrow of Love *a*
(First book version, 1892)

I
,The quarrel *b* of the sparrows in the eaves,
,The full round moon and the star-laden sky,
,And the loud song of the ever-singing leaves *c*
,Had hid *d* away earth's old and weary *e* cry.

II
,And then you came with those red mournful lips,
,And with you came the whole of the world's tears,
,And all the sorrows *f* of her labouring ships
,And all the burden *g* of her myriad *h* years.

---

a *1892 Ind*: the World
b *1892 Ind*: quarreling
c *1895*: leaves,
d *1891*: hushed
e *1892 Ind*: bitter
f *1892 Ind*: sorrow; *1895*: trouble
g *1895*: trouble
h *1891*: million

₁And now the sparrows warring*i* in the eaves,

III   ₂The crumbling*j* moon, the white*k* stars in the sky,

₃And the loud chaunting of the unquiet leaves,*l*

₄Are shaken with earth's old and weary*e* cry.

2.3   Actually, the poem offers two profoundly different texts, the early version of 1892, with a series of variants from the manuscript of 1891 to the final retouchings of 1895, and, on the other hand, the last, radically revised version of 1925. The final revision was so extensive that the vocabulary of the two versions has in common only: 1) the rhyme-words — in a few cases with their antecedent auxiliary words (I ₁ *in the eaves*, ₂*and *** the *** sky*, ₃*of *** leaves*, ₄*and *** cry*; III ₃ *of the *** leaves*, ₄*and *** cry*) and with the exception of one substitution (1925: II ₄*peers* for *1892: years*) — or with their attributes in the inner quatrain (II ₁ *red mournful*, ₃ *labouring*); 2) seven initial accessory monosyllables (five *and*, two *the*, one *had*); 3) one noun inside the second line of each quatrain (I ₂ *moon*, II ₂ *world*, III ₂ *moon*).

---

i *1891*: angry sparrows; *1892 Ind*: warring sparrows
j *1891* and *1892 Ind*: withered; *1895*: curd-pale
k *1892 Ind*: pale
l *1891*: The wearisome loud chaunting of the leaves,

COMPOSITION

3.0   The poem consists of three quatrains which in their structure display two patent binary oppositions: the two outer quatrains (I and III) exhibit common properties distinct from those of the inner quatrain (II), while at the same time they differ essentially in their internal structure from each other.

3.1   Both in the early and final version the poem confronts two opposite levels of subject matter, the upper and lower respectively. Six lines are devoted to each of them. The upper sphere, which may be labeled the 'overground' level, is treated in the first three lines of each outer quatrain. The lower level is focused upon in the four lines of the inner quatrain and in the fourth line of each outer quatrain. The last line of these two quatrains (I_4 and III_4) designates its topic as *earth* in the early version of the poem and as *man* in the late version, and the lower level may thus be defined as 'terrestrial' in respect to *SL 1892* and as specifically 'human' in *SL 1925*.

3.20   Only the outer quatrains expressly designate the two different levels and bring them into conflict. In both versions of the poem the initial quatrain portrays the outcome of this combat as a victory, and the final quatrain — as a defeat, of the overground level. Yet the extent of these outcomes varies significantly in the two versions of the poem. In the early version (*SL 1892*) the two rival levels continue to coexist, and only their hierarchy undergoes a change: at the beginning the overground I_4*Had hid away earth's old and weary cry*, but at the end it is the characters of the overground who III_4*Are shaken with earth's *** cry*. To this preserved contiguity of the adversary spheres the late version of the poem (*SL 1925*) replies first by the obliteration of the human level (the overground I_4*Had blotted out man's image and his cry*) and then, conversely, by the dissolution of the overground in the human level (the characters of the upper level III $_4$ *Could but compose man's image and his cry*). (In the parlance of the French translator Yves Bonnefoy, "Ne purent être qu'à l'image de l'homme et son cri d'angoisse", and in R. Exner's German translation, "Verdichten sich zu Menschenruf und Menschenbild". As indicated by *A Concordance to the Poems of W. B. Yeats*, the verb *compose* appears in Yeats' poetry but once, in the final line of *SL 1925* [Parrish, p. 159].)

3.21 The mere contiguity, definable in metonymic terms, which characterized the two spheres in the outer quatrains of *SL 1892*, in *SL 1925* turns into a mutual metamorphosis of two contrastive sets of givens. The alternation of auditory and visual phenomena which delineate the upper sphere remains valid in both versions (the noise of the sparrow, the celestial view, the sound of leaves), but in the early version is contrasted with the merely audible aspect of the lower sphere, whereas in *SL 1925* the latter follows a similar differentiation (*image* and *cry*), whereby the lower sphere becomes deployed in conformance with the twofold nature of the overground level.

3.3 In the inner quatrain of *SL 1925*, the heroine who suddenly emerges (II $_1$ *A girl arose*) is identified —through a chain of similies (II $_2$ *seemed*, $_3$ *like*, $_4$ *as*) —with the tragic and heroic human world. The system of metaphors underlying the inner quatrain of *SL 1925* differs patently from the whimsical metathetic confrontation of the two sociative prepositions *with* (II $_1$ *And then you came with****, $_2$ *And with you came****) in *SL 1892* and from the series of summarizing totalizers (II $_2$ *the whole of****, $_3$ *And all the*** of****, $_4$ *And all the*** of****) in the early version. The first of these totalizers (II $_2$ *the whole of the world's tears*) was transformed in *SL 1925* into II $_2$ *the greatness of the world in tears*, which is in rough semantic contrast with I $_2$ *The brawling of a sparrow in the eaves*, while at the same time demonstrating an expressive formal parallelism that further emphasizes the irreconcilable divergences between the two levels.

3.4 To the simultaneous concord and discord between the parts of each of the integral poems, Yeats' creed as poet and creative visionary adds a different fusion of stability and variability namely his view of development as "a temporal image of that which remains in itself", to quote Hegel as cited by the poet (*Vision*, p. 249). The two kinds of continual conflict between being and its opposite encompass both 'coexistence' and 'succession' according to Yeats, and in the case under discussion this applies to the dramatic tension both between the inner and outer or initial and final stanzas within one version of the poem and between the poem in its two different versions, the latter of which is seen by the author on the one hand as an "altogether new" poem (*Var.*, p.842) and on the other hand as still belonging "to the time when [it was] first written" (*Var.*, p. 855). Like the individual stanzas of *SL 1892* or *1925*, which find their antithesis within the given version, these two versions in turn stand next to each other in an antithetical struggle and harmonious complementarity.

3.5   In the "Dedication" to his *Early Poems and Stories* (1925) Yeats concludes his comments on the new versions of some poems "written before his seven-and-twentieth year" with the conviction: "I have found a more appropriate simplicity" (*Var.*, p. 855). Critics, with rare exceptions (see R. Cowell 1969:144), have repudiated the alteration of *SL* with such statements as: "the new version as a whole is both ill-digested and obscure" (MacNeice 1941:71); "the poem has been emptied of its vital content" (Hone 1943:126); the earlier versions of *SL* "were inherently more logical and less pretentious and hence more charming" (Saul 1957:56). It seems necessary to replace such unsubstantiated polemical replies to the poet's own view by a detailed and objective comparison of Yeats' poem in its two phases.

GRAMMAR

4.0   It is against the background of the manifest grammatical symmetry underlying and uniting the three quatrains — and this symmetry is indeed supreme in *SL 1925* — that the significant individuality of each stanza in the dramatic composition of the entire poem gains a particular potency and eloquence. The distinct and thematically related features which differentiate single quatrains, their distichs, and single lines are achieved either through appreciable deviations from the predominant morphological and syntactic matrices or through the filling of these matrices with semantically divergent lexical and phraseological constituents. Robert Frost's metaphor, a favorite of I. A. Richards, on poets' preference for playing tennis with a net is valid not only for meter and rhyme but for the grammatical pattern of a poem as well.

-*ING*-FORMS

1925

5.0   Before focusing on the two basic grammatical opposites — noun and verb — let us mention the intermediate morphological entity which is, according to Strang (1968:175), "best labelled non-committally the *-ing-form*". Such forms appear once in every stanza of *SL 1925*, each time introducing the motif of movement into the nominal part of the three sentences: the first, in a substantival function, I ₁*The brawling*, and the other two in an adjectival use, II ₃*the labouring ships* and III ₂*A climbing moon.*

1891–1892

5.1   Like *SL 1925*, the manuscript of 1891 contained one *-ing*-form in each quatrain, two of the three in adjectival and one in substantival function (I ₃*ever-singing*, II ₃*labouring*, III ₃*the**** *chaunting*). Their salient pattern in *SL 1891* was their location in the third line of each quatrain. *SL 1892* displays a greater tendency toward dynamism in the third quatrain, in which, besides the already-mentioned substantival III ₃*the**** *chaunting*, one finds the two attributes ₁*warring* and ₂*crumbling*.

NOUNS

1925

6.0   The poem contains twenty seven (3^3) nouns, nine (3^2) in each quatrain, of which three in each quatrain occur with prepositions:

I $_1$(of) *sparrow*, (in) *eaves*; $_2$*moon, sky*; $_3$*harmony*, (of) *leaves*; $_4$*man's image, cry*.

II $_1$*girl, lips*; $_2$*greatness*, (of) *world*, (in) *tears*; $_3$*Odysseus, ships*; $_4$*Priam*, (with) *peers*.

III $_1$(on) *instant, eaves*; $_2$*moon*, (upon) *sky*; $_3$*lamentation*, (of) *leaves*; $_4$*man's, image, cry*.

6.1   One even line of each quatrain has three nouns (I$_4$, II$_2$, III$_4$), and any other line — two nouns. This rule can be further specified. In the outer (odd) quatrains the even line of the even distich contains an odd number of nouns (3), whereas in the inner (even) quatrains this odd number of nouns (3) is found in the even line of the odd distich. Any other line of the poem contains an even number of nouns (2).

6.2   Each quatrain has only one abstract noun, each of more than one syllable and each followed by the same preposition: I $_3$*harmony* (of); II $_2$*greatness* (of); III $_3$*lamentation* (of).

6.3   The poem contains six personal (human, i.e. belonging to the *who*-gender) nouns, of which two common (II $_1$*girl*, $_4$*peers*) and two proper names ($_3$*Odysseus*, $_4$*Priam*) appear in the inner quatrain, whereas each of the outer quatrains has only one personal noun, the possessive *man's* in I$_4$ and III$_4$. Of these six personal nouns only one (II $_1$*girl*) belongs to the feminine (*she*-) gender, while the other five are of the masculine (*he*-) gender.

6.40 Only nouns function as rhyme-fellows, and the plural occurs solely in rhymes: eight of the twelve rhyme-fellows are plural nouns. Might not this propensity of the rhyming line-ends for the plural perhaps underscore a contrast between the frame of the lines and their inside? Is not the inside of the line the actual arena in which the individual actors of the drama perform, such as 'the brawling sparrow' and 'the brilliant moon', 'a girl' and 'man', 'Odysseus' and 'Priam'?

6.41 The distinctness of the rhymes is highlighted not only by their grammatical peculiarities, but also by the consistent use of monosyllabic words in all the rhymes of the poem and by the common vocalic properties that all of them share: the rhymes of the first quatrain, all repeated in the third, are built on the phoneme /i/ alone or as the asyllabic end of the diphthong /ai/, while all four lines of the second quatrain use /I/, the lax (short) opposite of the tense /i/.

6.42 The two constituents of each of the six rhymes are morphologically homogeneous but syntactically heterogeneous. In each quatrain one line ends in a grammatical subject (I $_2$*sky*, II $_3$*ships*, III $_1$*eaves*), one in a direct object (I $_4$*cry*, II $_1$*lips*, III $_4$*cry*), and two in prepositional constructions (I $_1$*in the eaves*, $_3$*of leaves*; II $_2$*in tears*, $_4$*with his peers*; III $_2$*upon an empty sky*, $_3$*of the leaves*).

6.43 The variety in the syntactic use of the rhyming nouns achieved in *SL 1925* is lacking in the early version, where ten of the rhyme-fellows belong to prepositional constructions. The only exception in *SL 1892* is the rhyming of the subject I $_2$*sky* with the direct object I $_4$*cry*, which grammatically underlines the striking opposition of the overground and terrestrial levels (cf. 3.2ff. above).

1892

6.5 The distribution of nouns is here less symmetrical than in the final version. There is a total of 25 nouns in *SL 1892*, the number per quatrain oscillating between nine (I) and eight (II and III). One line of each quatrain contains three nouns; two lines — two nouns each; and one line — two or one.

6.6 All three abstract nouns of *SL 1925* are innovations of the final version; the early version is completely devoid of abstracts. There are no properly personal nouns, but *SL 1892* contains three possessive forms, each in an even line of a different quatrain and each pertaining to a noun which exhibits, in Jespersen's terms (1924:237), "some approach to personification": II $_2$ *the world's tears* and I $_4$, III $_4$ *earth's cry*, the latter in positional correspondence to the possessive form of the properly personal noun in *SL 1925*, I $_4$, III $_4$ *man's*. (As regards the personalization of the possessives of *SL 1892*, cf. such lines in Yeats' works as "The wandering earth *herself***" [*Var.*, 65, line 18] or "before earth took him to *her* stony care" [*Var.*, 126, line 4]). It is noteworthy that in both versions the possessive always falls on the metrical upbeat (cf. 17.30ff.). The increase of personalization among the nouns of *SL 1925* is also witnessed by the replacement of the personal pronoun *you* in II $_{1-2}$ of *SL 1892* by the noun II $_1$ *girl* (cf. 19.7)

6.7   The number of plurals in the rhyme-fellows remains constant in both versions, but *SL 1892* has, in addition, four plural nouns *inside* the line, one in quatrains I and II, and two in quatrain III: I $_1$ *sparrows*; II $_3$ *sorrows*, III $_1$ *sparrows*, $_2$ *stars*. All four interior plurals are framed by hissing sibilants, an initial /s/ and a final /z/, and have a stressed vowel followed by /r/. Thus the grammatical differentiation between the inside and the end of the lines achieved in *SL 1925* by the restriction of plural nouns to the latter (cf. 6.40) is missing in *SL 1892*.

6.8   The word *sorrows* of II $_3$ was apparently discarded in the final version to avoid the repetition of the words of the title within the text, as in a similar way the tentative title of *SL 1892 Ind*, "The Sorrow of the World" was cancelled because *world*, not *love*, occurs in the text. The pun-like confrontation of II $_3$ *sorrows* and I $_1$, III $_1$ *sparrows* became confined in *SL 1925* to the title and opening line, where *sparrows* imitate the singular form of *Sorrow*. This change from plural to singular, effective not only in grammatical meaning but also in sound (cf. 16.2 below) — I $_1$ *The brawling of a sparrow*** — met with the objections of the critic Parkinson (1951:168), for whom "*brawling* is not perfectly right: can one sparrow brawl?". Cf., however, such usages of this word in Yeats' poetry as "big brawling lout" (*Var.*, 301, line 9) or "I took you for a brawling ghost" (*Var.*, 304, variant to line 41).

PRENOMINAL ATTRIBUTES

1925

7.0 The phrases built of nouns and prenominal attributes (adjectives proper and -*ing*-forms) in the three quatrains of *SL 1925* display a remarkably symmetrical patterning:

	LINE:	1.	2.	3.	4.	TOTAL
	I:	—	2	1	— =	3
QUATRAIN	II:	2	—	1	— =	3
	III:	1	2	—	— =	3
						9

7.1 Each quatrain contains two lines with and two lines without prenominal attributes. There are no prenominal attributes in the fourth line of any quatrain. Of the first three lines in each quatrain, one line contains two, one line — one, and one line — no prenominal attributes. The third line contains no more than one prenominal attribute (I $_3$*famous*, II $_3$*labouring*, III $_3$——). If one of the first three lines contains no prenominal attributes, a neighboring line will have two of them: I $_1$——, $_2$*brilliant, milky*; II $_1$*red, mournful*, $_2$——; III $_2$*climbing, empty*, $_3$——). In contradistinction to the outer quatrains, with prenominal attributes in contiguous lines, the inner quatrain has such attributes in its odd lines only. The line without prenominal attributes advances from one quatrain to the next, so that its distribution forms a descending curve. The distribution of prenominal attributes in the first three lines of the final quatrain displays a mirror symmetry to that of the initial quatrain (1, 2, – $\leftrightarrow$ –, 2, 1).

1892

7.2   The early version of *SL* is almost twice as rich in prenominal attributes with an epithetical function (total 17–18) and has a higher number of such attributes in the outer as opposed to the inner quatrains: seven in I ($_2$ *full round,* $_2$ *star-laden,* $_3$ *loud,* $_3$ *ever-singing,* $_4$ *old and weary*) and seven in the earliest two versions of III (*1891* and *1892 Ind*), whereas the number in *SL 1892* is reduced to six — $_2$ *crumbling,* $_2$ *white,* $_3$ *loud,* $_3$ *unquiet,* $_4$ *old and weary* — by the replacement of the prenominal attribute *1891: angry* (*1892 Ind: warring*) *sparrows* by III $_1$ *sparrows warring.* On the other hand, II contains only four prenominal attributes: $_1$ *red mournful,* $_3$ *labouring,* $_4$ *myriad.*

7.3   One could say that the changes found in *SL 1925* are in line with such slogans as Marianne Moore's warning against the use of too many adjectives and adverbs, which is based upon the notion that "poetry is all nouns and verbs" (*New York Times*, March 22, 1962, p. 31). As Parkinson states, the revised text of the poem "reduces the number and sensuous reference of epithets" (1951:172). Yeats himself acknowledges a tendency toward the exfoliation of his style (*Auto.*, p. 291).

POSTPOSITIVE ATTRIBUTES

8.0 *SL 1925* contains postpositive (semi-predicative) attributes only in the second distich of the inner quatrain (cf. 15.0). Of the three occurrences, two are past passive participles (II $_3$*Doomed,* $_4$*murdered*) and one is an adjective (II $_4$*proud*). The only postpositive attribute in *SL 1892* (III $_1$*sparrows* WARRING *in the eaves*) was absent in the two earliest variants (*1891,1892 Ind*).

PRONOUNS

1925

9.0 Only three pronouns occur in the poem. All three are attributive, and each of them — *his, that, all* — is repeated three times, giving a sum total of nine. *His* occupies the penultimate syllable of the last line in each quatrain and refers expressly to a masculine noun: I $_4$*his cry*, II $_4$*his peers*, III $_4$*his cry* (*man's* in I$_4$ and III$_4$; *Priam* in II$_4$). *That* appears in one odd line of each quatrain, as a demonstrative pronoun referring, in a rather high-flown manner, to abstracts in the outer quatrains (I $_3$*that* *** *harmony*, III $_3$*that lamentation*) and as a relative pronoun referring to a feminine noun in the inner quatrain (II $_1$*a girl* *** *that*) — in accordance with the subordinative structure of this stanza (cf. 14.1). *All* occurs only in the outer quatrains, two times in contiguous lines of the first and once in the third, in the combinations *and all the* (I$_2$), *And all that* (I$_3$, III$_3$), and refers to singular nouns of the overground level, I $_2$*sky*, I $_3$*harmony of leaves*, III $_3$*lamentation of the leaves*.

1892

9.1 The outer quatrains of *SL 1892* are devoid of pronouns, whereas the inner quatrain contains seven. In *SL 1925* Yeats "dropped the simulation of the structure of address" (Parkinson 1951:168), while all the early versions of *SL* twice make use of the personal pronoun *you* in the first distich, with reference to the female addressee of the poem, and then of *her* in the second distich, with reference to the *world*, which merges with the addressee: II $_1$*you came with* *** $_2$*And with you came the whole of the world's tears*. All the lines of the inner quatrain are dominated by the *she*-gender, which is directly expressed in both lines of the second distich and clearly alluded to in the *you* and *world* of the first distich (cf. 6.6 above). In *SL 1925* the feminine pronoun of the first distich (the relative *that* of II $_1$) gives way to the masculine pronoun of the second distich (II $_4$*his*), and the division into two distichs contrasted in gender is supported by the distribution of feminine and masculine nouns (II $_1$*girl* and $_2$*world* vs. $_3$*Odysseus*, $_4$*Priam*, *peers*). Twice, in turn, the pronoun *all* opens the contiguous lines of the second distich in the inner quatrain of *SL 1892* (II $_{3,4}$*And all the* ***), where it refers to nouns of the terrestrial level (II $_3$*sorrows*, $_4$*burdens*); in *SL 1925* this pronoun is found, on the contrary, in the *outer* quatrains (I $_3$, III $_3$*And all that* ***), where it refers to the *overground* level (cf. 9.0 above). Finally, II $_1$ *those*, in the context *you came with those red mournful lips*, reinforces the odic manner of direct address in the early version and makes the roles of both the addresser and the addressee more prominent (cf. 19.7).

ADVERBS

10.0   Two adverbs, II $_1$*then* and III $_1$*now*, each preceded by the initial conjunction *And*, open the two sentences of the second and third quatrains of *SL 1892* (note also a third adverbial form in the first quatrain which is part of the complex adjective I $_3$*And *** ever-singing*). All three disappear in *SL 1925* (cf. 18.71 below).

ARTICLES

1925

11.0   The nine occurrences of *the* in the three quatrains form an arith-metical regression: 4 — 3 — 2. In the first half of the poem, three lines contain two definite articles each, and three —none, whereas the second half has three lines with one definite article in each, and three without any. In each quatrain of the poem, there are two lines with, and two without, definite articles.

		LINE:	1.	2.	3.	4.	TOTAL
	I:		2 *the*	2 *the*	—	—	4
QUATRAIN	II:		—	2 *the*	1 *the*	—	3
	III:		1 *the*	—	1 *the*	—	2
							9

Only one line in each quatrain, and in each case a different line, contains both the definite article and prenominal attributes: I_2, II_3, III_1. Each quatrain has one line with the indefinite article *a* and/or *an*, which may be compared to the equal distribution of lines with the definite article (2 lines per quatrain). The final line of each quatrain is completely devoid of articles.

11.1   The distribution of the articles is limited to the first two lines in the first quatrain and forms a rectangle. In the second and third quat-rains the articles extend over the first three lines of each and form the figure of an oblique-angled quadrangle:

I:	*The*	*a*	*the*
	The		*the*

II:	*A*		
	the		*the*
			the

III:	*The*		
	A		*an*
			the

1892

11.2 Of the articles, *a* is totally absent from *SL 1892*, whereas the distribution of the definite articles — 18 in the entire poem: seven in each of the outer quatrains and four in the inner one — corresponds strikingly to the identical pattern of prenominal attributes in the two earliest variants of the poem (cf. 7.2 above). It should be noted, finally, that in each quatrain of *SL 1892* only one line lacks the definite article: the final line in the outer quatrains, and the initial line in the inner quatrain.

CONNECTIVES

1925

12.0 The poem contains two equational conjunctions, both confined to the inner quatrain (II $_3$*like*, $_4$*as*), against nine copulative conjunctions, three instances of *and* in each quatrain. The other class of connectives, namely the prepositions (which here include *of*, *in*, *with*, *on*, and *upon*), like copulative conjunctions, numbers nine *in toto*, three per quatrain. The latter two classes of connectives taken together are attested nine times in each half of the poem (I_1–II_2 and II_3–III_4).

12.1 The distribution of these two categories (copulative conjunctions and prepositions) forms an identical chiasmus in the two distichs of each quatrain:

	CONJ.	+	PREP.	=	TOTAL
FIRST DISTICH:	1	chiasmus	2	=	3
SECOND DISTICH:	2		1	=	3
QUATRAIN	3		3	=	6

Thus in the transition from the first distich to the second each quatrain displays one and the same movement from government performed by the prepositions to grammatical agreement carried by the copulative conjunction *and*. This rule of transition from superposition to alignment may be juxtaposed to the consistent absence of masculine personal nouns in the first distichs of all three quatrains and the presence of such nouns in the final distich of each quatrain (cf. 6.3).

1892

12.2   Unlike *SL 1925*, the early version completely lacks equational conjunctions (cf. 3.3 above). As regards the copulative conjunctions and prepositions, their distribution in the two distichs of the first quatrain coincides with that of *SL 1925*. The tendency toward a higher number of prepositions in the first distich as opposed to the second is observable also in the other two quatrains of *SL 1892*, but the distribution is less regular than that of *SL 1925*, where the pattern established by the first quatrain was generalized throughout the poem. Thus, the distribution by distich exhibits the following pattern in *SL 1892* taken as a whole:

	CONJ.	+	PREP.	=	TOTAL
FIRST DISTICHS:	4		7	=	11
SECOND DISTICHS:	6		5	=	11
QUATRAINS:	10		12	=	22

In other words, the total number of all connectives throughout the early version of the poem is the same for its odd and even distichs. This equality is strengthened in *SL 1925* by the equal number of copulative conjunctions and prepositions in the poem as a whole and in each of its quatrains, and by the total number of such forms in each distich of the entire text (cf. 12.1 above).

THE SORROW OF LOVE

The brawling of a sparrow in the eaves,
The brilliant moon and all the milky sky,
And all that famous harmony of leaves,
Had blotted out man's image and his cry.

A girl arose that had red mournful lips
And seemed the greatness of the world in
   tears,
Doomed like Odysseus and the labouring
   ships
And proud as Priam murdered with his
   peers;

Arose, and on the instant clamorous eaves,
A climbing moon upon an empty sky,
And all that lamentation of the leaves,
Could but compose man's image and his cry.

The *Sorrow* of *Love.*

The quarrel of the sparrows in the eaves,
  The full round moon and the star-laden
    sky,
And the loud song of the ever-singing leaves
  Had hid away earth's old and weary cry.

And then you came with those red mournful lips,
  And with you came the whole of the world's
    tears,
And all the sorrows of her labouring ships,
  And all burden of her myriad years.

And now the sparrows warring in the eaves,
  The crumbling moon, the white stars in the
    sky,
And the loud chanting of the unquiet leaves,
  Are shaken with earth's old and weary cry.

FINITE VERBS

1925

13.0   In the first half of the poem three lines without finites (I_{1-3}) are followed by three lines each containing one or more finites (I_4-II_2); in the second half of the poem the last line of each three-line group (II_3-III_1, III_{2-4}) contains a finite.

13.1   The number of finites is limited to six active forms referring to the third person. Three of these forms (1 + 2) appear in the outer quatrains, and three — in the first distich of the inner quatrain. The ratio of verbs to nouns is 1:3 in the inner and 1:8 in the two outer quatrains.

13.2   All three semantic types of verbs outlined by Jespersen (1924:86)— verbs of action, of process, and of state — occur, each twice, among the six finite forms of *SL 1925*. The verbs of action are represented by two compound forms bound to the first hemistich of the last line in the outer quatrains (I_4*Had blotted out*, III_4*Could but compose*). The verbs of state are restricted to the first distich of the inner quatrain (II_1*had*, $_2$*And seemed*). The repeated verb of process occurs in the initial hemistich of the inner and last quatrains (II_1*arose*, III_1*Arose*). In *SL 1925* the verbs of action in their compound form each consist of four syllables, the verbs of process — two, and the verbs of state — of only one syllable.

13.3   The finites of the three quatrains exhibit a pervasive interplay. The initial and final predicates of the poem (I_4*Had blotted out*, III_4*Could but compose*), its only compound verbal forms and its only verbs of action, are dramatically played against one another. The auxiliary (I_4*Had****) yields patently to the independent appearance of the same verb (II_1*had *** lips*), which then pairs with the only other verb of status, II_2*And seemed ****. The only verb of process, *arose*, which heads the

whole sentence of the inner quatrain (II $_1$*A girl arose* ***), is repeated
to introduce the third quatrain (III $_1$*Arose, and****) and, finally, forms
an internal rhyme with the last verb of the poem, III $_4$ *** *compose*.

1892

13.4   *SL 1925* contains a higher number of finites and, at the same time,
exhibits a greater grammatical uniformity in their use than does the
early version. The repertory of verbs in *SL 1892* is limited to four finites,
two in the first distich of the inner quatrain and two in the last lines
of the outer quatrains. The ratio of verbs to nouns is here 1:4 in the
inner quatrain and 1:8 in the outer quatrains. The inner quatrain twice
uses the same preterit, *came*, first in reference to the second person
(II $_1$*you came with ***) and then in reference to the third person (II $_2$ *with*
*you came the whole ***). The compound finite forms of the outer quatrains, the sole verbs of action, differ in tense and voice (I $_4$ *Had hid away*,
III $_4$ *Are shaken*).

13.5   In contradistinction to *SL 1925*, the early version lacks verbs of
state. The verbs of action in the two versions are bound to the last line
of the outer quatrains, whereas the first distich of the inner quatrain
contains the verbs of process in *SL 1892* and the verbs of state in *SL 1925*.
The verb of process occurs twice in both the early and final version, but
in the former refers to different persons (second and third respectively)
and in the latter qualifies as a genuine repetition (referring in both
instances to II $_1$*A girl*). In *SL 1925* this verb of process pertains to the
initial hemistich of the inner and final quatrains, while in *SL 1892* it is
attached to the initial hemistich of the first and second line of the inner
quatrain.

13.6.   Despite these variations, the different semantic types of verbs
follow the same mirror symmetry in both versions:

	1925	1892
Action	*Had blotted out*	*Had hid away*
Process	*arose*	*came*
State	*had*	
State	*seemed*	
Process	*Arose*	*came*
Action	*Could but compose*	*Are shaken*

COORDINATION AND SUBORDINATION
OF CLAUSES

1925

14.0   The substantial difference between the inner quatrain and the two outer ones lies in their syntactic organization. The first and third quatrains are built on a coordination of four elliptical clauses: I a) ₁*The brawling**** [*Had blotted out****]; b) ₂*The brilliant moon* [*Had blotted out*****]; c) ₂*and all the milky sky* [*Had blotted out*****]; d) ₃*And**** that harmony**** ₄Had blotted out man's image and his cry*; III a) [*a girl*] ₁*Arose*; b) ₁*and**** eaves* [*Could but compose*****]; c) ₂*A***** moon**** [*Could but compose*****]; d) ₃*And**** that lamentation***** ₄Could but compose man's image and his cry.*

14.1   In the inner stanza, on the contrary, the syntactic division into four parts is based on grammatical subordination: II a) ₁*A girl arose*; b) ₁*that had**** ₂And seemed*****; c) ₃*Doomed**** ₄And proud*****; d) ₄ *murdered***** (cf. 15.0). Each of the two inner parts of this quatrain — b) and c) — is in turn divided into two coordinate sections, each of which is bound together by the conjunction *and.*

1892

14.2   Each of the outer quatrains forms a sentence of four coordinated subjects bound elliptically with one and the same predicate: I a) ₁ *The quarrel***** [*Had hid away*****] b) ₂*The **** moon* [*Had hid away*****]; c) ₂*and **** the **** sky* [*Had hid away*****]; d) ₃*And the **** song **** ₄Had hid away earth's old and weary cry*; III a) ₁*And now the sparrows*****; b) ₂*The***** moon ****; c)₂the***** stars *****;d) ₃Andthe***** chaunting***** ₄Are shaken with earth's old and weary cry.* In contradistinction to *SL 1925*, in the early version the inner quatrain also forms a coordinate sentence, which consists of a complete initial clause — a) II $_1$*And then you came* *** — followed by an elliptical combination of one predicate with three consequent subjects — b) $_2$*And with you came the whole* ***; c) $_3$*And* [*with you came*] *all the sorrows* *** ; d) $_4$*And* [*with you came*] *all the burden* ***.

14.3   Thus in *SL 1892* coordination remains the constructive principle within each of the three quatrains, whereas *SL 1925* opposes the outer, coordinate quatrains to the inner quatrain, which is built on the principle of subordination (cf. 19.5).

PREDICATION

1925

15.0   In the outer quatrains of both the early and final version, all the nominal subjects of the first three lines await their predicate in the fourth line. In the inner quatrain of *SL 1925* the main clause — II $_1$ *A girl arose* — takes up the initial hemistich of the first line, but the rest of the first distich is occupied by two collaterally subordinated clauses whose different predicates relate to the same antecedent subject, whereas in the outer quatrains different coordinated subjects relate to one and the same final predicate. In the second distich of this inner quatrain the two lines begin with semi-predicates of contracted collateral clauses (II $_3$ *Doomed* — $_4$ *And proud*) which are subordinated to an antecedent headword and followed in the final hemistich by a participial clause of lower syntactic rank (II $_4$ *murdered with his peers*).

1892

15.1   The basic structural difference between the inner quatrain of *SL 1892* and its outer quatrains lies in the progressive direction of the latter as opposed to the regressive orientation of the former (on these terms cf. Halliday 1963 and Yngve 1961). Although the inner quatrain is composed, like the outer quatrains, of coordinated subjects with a joint predicate, there is an essential difference in the order of the primaries: in the outer quatrains the predicate is placed after the subject, whereas in the inner it appears before them (II $_2$ **** came the whole*** $_3$ And all the sorrows*** $_4$ And all the burden*). In the terms of *A Vision*, "these pairs of opposites [subject and predicate] whirl in contrary directions" (p. 74). The same may be said of the distinctive criterion for the opposition of inner versus outer quatrains in *SL 1925*, i.e. the principle of subordination as opposed to that of coordination (cf. 14.3 above).

15.2   Each of the two versions of *SL* contains one deviation from the opposition between the inner and outer quatrains established by the expression of subject and predicate. In *SL 1892* the first clause of the inner quatrain is the only one in the stanza which places the predicate after the subject (II ₁*And then you came****). In *SL 1925* the initial, elliptical clause of the third quatrain, III ₁*Arose*, referring to the subject II ₁*A girl*, is the only one among the elliptic clauses of the stanza which omits the subject rather than the predicate. It is significant that in both versions of *SL* the deviation occurs in regard to the only verb which is twice repeated and which signals the appearance of the heroine.

SOUNDS

16.0   According to Yeats' meditation of 1900, "all sounds, all colours, all forms, either because of their preordained energies or because of long association, evoke indefinable and yet precise emotions, or, as I prefer to think, call down among us certain disembodied powers, whose footsteps over our hearts we call emotions" ("The Symbolism of Poetry", in *Essays*, 156f.).

16.1   The phonological association established in the early version of *SL* between the title of the lyric and the auditory imagery of its first quatrain is maintained in *SL 1925*: *Sorrow* — I $_1$*sparrow*, and *Love* — I $_3$*leaves*. Within the twelve lines of the poem the interplay of words allied in sound creates an affinity and contrast either between the components of the same line or between diverse lines within the same quatrain, and even within the same distichs, or, conversely, between correlative lines of two different quatrains. The appearance of expressive consonantal clusters through the use of tightly-knit word groups and of vocalic syncope furthers and widens the application of this poetic device.

16.2   Among other reasons for the textual changes in the final version of the outer quatrains (cf. 19.10 below), a pertinent role belongs to the paronomastic link established in these two stanzas between the auditory performance reported in their first lines and the visual phenomena referred to in their second lines. Moreover, especially in the first quatrain, a distinct alliteration binds these two vocables of the first distich, oriented respectively toward hearing and sight, with the predicate of the fourth line: I $_1$*brawling* /br.l/ — $_2$*brilliant* /br.l/ — $_4$*Had blotted* /bl/, and III $_1$*clamorous* /kl.m/ — $_2$*climbling* /kl.m/ — $_2$*empty* /mp/ — $_3$*lamentation* /l.m/ — $_4$*Could but compose* /k.mp/. The junctural cluster /db/ is common to both final predicates of the outer quatrains (I $_4$*Had blotted out* — III ₄*Could but*). Note also the similar juncture /tk/ of III ₁*instant clamorous* — III ₄*but compose*. It is worth mentioning that none of the quoted words occurred in the early version.

16.3   *Moon*, the significant verbal image which in all variants of *SL* heads the second line of the two outer stanzas (cf. 19.21f. below), finds no further support for its initial /m/ all through the first quatrain of the early version, and the only complementary instance of /m/ in the third quatrain — III ₂*crumbling moon* of *SL 1892* —was replaced in all editions from 1895 to 1924 by the nasal-less epithet *curd-pale*. Yet the latter form maintains the /k/, /r/, /l/ of its antecedent (which must have had an influence even on the sound shape and suffix of the corresponding attribute *climbing* in *SL 1925*). The chromatic and paronomastic correspondence to III ₂*The curd-pale* /rd. . .1/ or *crumbling* /r.m.1/ *moon* was enclosed in the II ₁*red mournful* /r.dm. . .1/ *lips* of the inner quatrain with three further enhancing occurrences of /m/: II ₁,₂*came* and ₄*myriad* (cf. 16.8 and 19.30). The focal innovation of *SL 1925* in its outer quatrains was the providing of ₂*moon* with its vocalic, grammatical (*he*-gender), and semantic counterpart in the other even line of the same stanzas — I₄ and III ₄*man's* (cf. 19.11).

16.4   In the outer quatrains of *SL 1925* the abstracts of the third, intermediate line — I ₃*harmony* /m.n/ and III ₃*lamentation* /m.n/ — throw a paronomastic bridge between I, III ₂*moon* and ₄*man's*; at the same time they intensify the antithetic relation between the inner and outer stanzas, whereas in *SL 1892* the final distichs of the outer quatrains repeatedly confront I ₃*the loud* /1.d/ *song* (or III ₃*chaunting*) *of the*** leaves* with I ₄ and III ₄*earth's old* /.1d/ *and weary cry*.

16.5   In *SL 1925* the even lines of the outer quatrains, in contradistinction to the odd lines, possess a clear-cut masculine break after the second downbeat of the iambic pentameter. In the outer quatrains the first hemistich of the second line finishes with *moon*, and the second hemistich of the fourth line begins with *man's*. The initial /m/ of the two alternants is symmetrically reinforced by the phonemic environment. In contradistinction to the only couple of grave (labial) nasals in *SL 1895* and subsequent editions before 1925 (I₂ and III ₂*moon*), the outer quatrains of *SL 1925* number fourteen instances of this phoneme: within the initial quatrain /m/ appears twice in each of its even lines and in the intermediate line (I ₂*moon *** milky sky*, ₄*man's image*,

₃*famous harmony*); the final quatrain has one /m/ in each odd line and three in each even line (III ₁*clamorous,* ₂*climbing moon*** empty sky,* ₃*lamentation,* ₄*compose man's image*). The double chain of the /m.n/ responses is most telling: I *moon — harmony — man's*; III *moon — lamentation — man's*. It is also significant that precisely the final picture of the lonesome lunar wanderer contains the greatest accumulation of nasals: III ₂*A climbing moon upon an empty sky* (with seven nasals: three labial, three dental and one velar).

16.6   In the initial simile of the inner quatrain the sounds of the 'tenor', II ₁*girl* /g.rl/, show twofold ties with the 'vehicle', II ₂*greatness* /gr/ *of the world* /rl/. Let us mention in this connection that Marjorie Perloff was right in pointing out the 'trilled *r*'s' in the poet's recorded readings of his own poems (1970:29); the r-colored vowels of English include a postvocalic /r/ in Yeats' sound pattern, so that the vowel of *girl* and *world* is here really followed by a pair of liquid phonemes /rl/. The seven occurrences of a tautosyllabic /r/ distinctly detach the inner quatrain of *SL 1925* from the outer quatrains, where /r/, with one exception (I ₃*harmony*), regularly occupies a prevocalic position.

16.7   The only internal noun common to both versions of the second stanza — II ₂*world* — is in both of them supplied with an antecedent analogous in its sonorant cluster /rl/: in *SL 1925* the preceding line of the same quatrain opens with the noun II ₁*girl*, whereas in *SL 1892* the corresponding line of the initial quatrain has two complex epithets each containing a cluster of these liquids — I ₂*full round* /1r/ ****star-laden* /rl/ — echoed by /rl/ in II ₃*her lab(ou)ring****.

16.8   In the inner quatrain of *SL 1925*, two subordinate constructions, the first and last not only in this stanza but also in the poem as a whole, are bound together by their melancholy mood and form a complex paronomasia: II ₁*had red mournful**** — ₄*murdered* /dr. dm.r — m.rd.rd/. It is curious that Parkinson (1951:169) scourned the latter "major word" as prosaic, unordered, and unable to "participate in the alliterative pattern": II ₄*proud* /pr/ — *Priam* /pr/ — *peers* /p.r/. An alliterative pattern concludes each outer quatrain in *SL 1892* (I ₃*harmony* — ₄*Had* — ₄*his,* III ₄*Could* — *compose* — *cry*), along with a triple vocalic 'anlaut': I ₄*away earth's old* and III ₄*Are shaken with earth's old****. Furthermore, one observes that although it does not take part in the alliteration of the initial consonants, II₄ *murdered* in *SL 1925* is nevertheless tied to the

words of the antecedent hemistich: *proud* /pr.d/ — /rd.rd/ and *Priam*
/pr.m/ — /m.r/. The two marginal lines of the inner quatrain inspired
Yeats from *SL 1892* on to seek a paronomastic bond in their somber
imagery: II ₁*mournful* /m.r/ *lips* — ₄*myriad* /m.r/ *years*. In *SL 1925* both
of these lines are patently framed in their sound shape by the imagery of
the surrounding distichs: I ₃*harmony of leaves* /rm.n...1/ — II ₁*red mourn-*
ful lips /r.dm.rn..1/ — II ₄*murdered* /m.rd.rd/ — III ₁*clam(o)rous eaves*
/1.mr/.

16.9   The only epithets taken over from the early version of the poem by
SL 1925 are those attached to the rhyme-words of the odd lines in the
inner quatrain: II ₁*red mournful lips* and ₃*lab(ou)ring ships*. The latter
attribute shared its sounds /1.br/ with II ₄*burden* /b.r/ of *SL 1892* and
II ₃,₄*trouble* /r.b.1/ of *SL 1895*. In *SL 1925* the inward antithesis (*a spar-*
row — the world) of the outwardly similar lines I₁ and II₂ (*the*** of****
in***; cf. 3.3 above) bursts into the utmost semantic contrast between
the chirp of a single little bird and the heavy scend of Odysseus' ships:
I ₁*brawling* — II ₃*lab(ou)ring*, tied together by the common suffix -*ing*
and by their identical but differently ordered root consonants /br.1/ —
/1.br/. The same lines of these two quatrains were juxtaposed in *SL 1892*
by the pun-like paronomasia I ₁*of the sparrows* — II ₃*the sorrows of* (cf.
6.8).

VERSE PATTERN

17.0 A detailed structural analysis of the masculine iambic pentameter in which *SL* is written would obviously require a careful examination of the poet's and his contemporaries' output in the same and cognate meters. Except for a few preliminary sketches by Dougherty (1973) and Bailey (1975), a systematic, linguistically-based inquiry into modern English versification has scarcely even begun, as compared to at least six decades of Slavic, especially Russian, investigation in the domain of metrics, with its historically and methodologically fruitful results in such questions as the rhythmical relevance of word boundaries and of higher syntactic units of varying rank.

17.1 For the main topic of our study — the comprehensive investigation of the basic oppositions which determine the relation, on the one hand, between the different parts of the poem in each version and, on the other, between *SL 1892* and *SL 1925* — the most illuminating aspect of the verse is the various patterning of the two fundamental prosodic types of words which fulfill the downbeats of the binary meter. These two types have been clearly distinguished both in the Russian tradition of metrical studies and in the most recent papers devoted to English versification. Thus P. Kiparsky singles out (1975:581), on the one hand, "members of lexical categories — nouns (including members of compounds), adjectives, verbs, and adverbs" and, on the other hand, "members of non-lexical categories (such as *his, the, and, with*)" which are in construction with the lexical members. (Russian tradition terms these two classes of units as 'lexical' and 'formal' respectively.) In *SL 1925*, for example, there is a significant difference between downbeats carrying the primary or only stress in the separate lexical constituents, e.g., I_2 *milky sky*, with two primary stresses, as opposed to I_3 *harmony*, with the primary stress on the first syllable, or I_1 *in the eaves*, with the primary stress on the third.

17.20   In *SL 1925* the outer quatrains display a clear regressive undulatory curve in the treatment of the downbeats: the three odd downbeats carry a greater percentage of primary stresses — and may thus be
designated as 'heavy' downbeats — than do the two even ('light') downbeats (see Figure 1). In these two outer quatrains, as in all stanzas of
SL irrespective of its version, the final downbeat of all lines is consis-
tently allotted a primary stress. In the initial quatrain of *SL 1925* all
three of the odd (heavy) downbeats receive a primary stress in all the
lines, whereas the fourth and second downbeats carry a primary stress
only in 1 and 2 lines respectively.

17.21   In the final quatrain the numerical superiority of primary
stresses on odd downbeats over the even downbeats remains valid, but
is reduced throughout, thus slightly flattening out the undulatory curve
exhibited in the initial quatrain: the first and third downbeats each
carry three primary stresses, and the second and fourth — two.

17.22   In opposition to the outer quatrains, with their sequence de-
scent/ascent (4–2–4 and 3–2–3), the inner quatrain displays the reverse

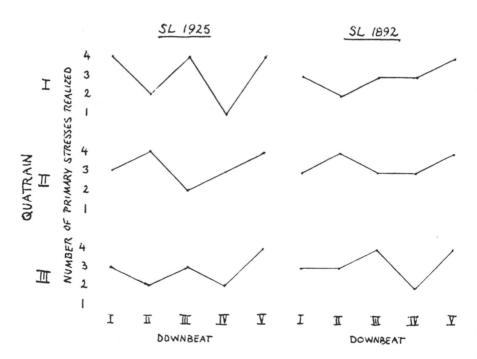

Fig. 1. Frequency of primary stresses on the downbeats in the two versions.

sequence (3–4–2), followed by a gradual ascent (3–4), so that it once again differs strikingly from the two outer quatrains (cf. particularly 18.30ff. below).

17.23 In *SL 1892*, as mentioned, the final downbeat of any line always carries a primary stress, but in the other four downbeats the undulatory curve is much less pronounced than in *SL 1925*: besides a sequence of descent and ascent, two neighboring downbeats may display an equal number of primary stresses. Thus there appears a mirror symmetry between the initial and final quatrain: descent — ascent — equality and equality — ascent — descent respectively (see Figure 1). The sequence equality — ascent (3–3–4), which concludes the order of downbeats in the initial and inner quatrains, opens the final quatrain. In terms of this relation, the inner quatrain of *SL 1892* occupies an intermediary place between the two outer quatrains.

17.30 Within the line, monosyllabic lexical words occur on upbeats and are followed by downbeats under primary stress 10 times in *SL 1892*, four times in each outer quatrain (with a consistent lexical symmetry between I and III: *moon — star — loud — earth's*), and two times in the inner quatrain: I $_2$*full round moon*, $_2$*star-laden*, $_3$*loud song*, $_4$*earth's old*; II $_1$*red mournful*, $_2$*world's tears*; III $_2$*curd-pale moon*, $_2$*white stars*, $_3$*loud chaunting*, $_4$*earth's old*.

17.31 Each quatrain of the final version preserves only one instance of the same phenomenon, literally repeating II $_1$*red mournful*, and replacing the possessive *earth's* by I$_4$ and III $_4$*man's*. The avoidance of fulfilling inner upbeats by stressed monosyllabic words approaches a rule.

17.4 Only *SL 1925* contains instances of the standard use of stressed monosyllables in the initial upbeat (anacrusis): II $_3$*Doomed like Odysseus*, III $_4$*Could but compose*.

CONSTRUCTIVE PRINCIPLES

1925

18.00   *SL 1925* displays an astounding symmetry in the distribution of the major grammatical categories among the three quatrains, a symmetry which is either lacking or muted in the early version. It may indeed be considered a persuasive example of the 'geometrical symbolism' (*Vision*, p. 80) which was so vital a force both in the poet's subliminal imagery and in his abstract thought. The operative principle regulating the poem's symmetries is here the number 3 and its exponents (3^2, 3^3). When reflecting on the 'Great Wheel' as the 'principal symbol' of the universe, Yeats insisted that "each set of 3 is itself a wheel" (*Vision*, p. 82f.). In his description of the 28 phases Yeats qualifies the first phase as "not being human" (*Vision*, p. 105), so that three to the third power (3^3) in fact exhausts the entire human realm.

18.01   There are 27 nouns *in toto* (3^3), 9 per quatrain (3^2), which include 3 abstracts and 3 nouns with prepositions, each distributed one per quatrain (cf. 6.0, 6.2). A total of three -*ing*-forms are present, one per quatrain (cf. 5.0). Prenominal attributes and pronouns each total 9 (3^2), the former distributed symmetrically (3 per quatrain; cf. 7.1), the latter displaying only partial symmetry (three different pronouns, two of which appear once in each quatrain; cf. 9.0). The occurrences of the definite article also total 9 (cf. 11.0). The connectives total 18, of which 9 (3^2) are copulative conjunctions and 9 (3^2) — prepositions, each appearing 3 times per quatrain (cf. 12.0). Only in the distribution of verbs does the principle of three find expression in a dichotomy of inner vs. outer stanzas rather than in their symmetrical equivalence (cf. 13.1).

1892

18.02   The impressive symmetrical identity established between the quatrains of *SL 1925* by the distribution of grammatical categories is almost entirely lacking in *SL 1892*. Of the major categories, only the possessives are equally apportioned, one per stanza (cf. 6.6). Instead of the equivalence symmetry of *SL 1925*, one finds in *SL 1892* a dissimilatory use of grammatical means to distinguish the inner from the two outer quatrains.

18.10   In *SL 1892* the contrast between the three quatrains is conveyed either by the presence of certain grammatical categories in the inner quatrain, coupled with their absence in I and III, or by an equal distribution of certain categories in the two outer quatrains as opposed to their lower frequency in the inner, and here it is the number 7, rather than 3, which serves as the operative principle.

   18.11   Thus, on the one hand, there are 7 pronouns in the inner quatrain, while the outer quatrains of *SL 1892* are completely devoid of this category (cf. 9.1). On the other hand, the inner quatrain has a lower number (4) of both prenominal attributes (cf. 7.2) and definite articles (cf. 11.2) than the outer quatrains, which each contain 7 such entities (but cf. 7.2).

   18.12   The inner quatrain of *SL 1892* also differs from the outer ones by the repetitive character of the initial part of the two lines within each distich (and their pronounced use of oxytones — cf. 19.41) and by the presence of redoubled grammatical words (the pronouns II $_{1,2}$*you*, $_{3,4}$*all*, $_{3,4}$*her* and the sociative prepositions $_{1,2}$*with*), which are lacking in the outer quatrains but are here strictly distributed by distich: II $_1$*And then* YOU *came* WITH *** — $_2$*And* WITH YOU *came* ***; $_{3,4}$*And* ALL *the* [$_3$*sorrows*, $_4$*burden*] *of* HER ***. (In *SL 1895* and subsequent editions before 1925 the parallelism of the line-beginnings in the second distich was complete: II $_{3,4}$*And all the trouble of her* ***.) The inner quatrain, moreover, is clearly dominated by the *she*-gender (cf. 9.1), which is merely hinted at in the last lines of the two outer quatrains (cf. 6.6).

   18.13   Finally, the inner quatrain of *SL 1892*, although it follows the principle of coordination displayed by the two outer quatrains, is differentiated from them in terms of predication. Whereas the two outer quatrains are built on a progressive principle of four coordinated subjects bound elliptically to one and the same final verb, the inner quatrain opens with one complete 'subject-predicate' clause, but then in the second line reverses the order of primaries into a sequence 'predicate-subject' (see 14.2).

18.2   It is worth noting that the two versions in several instances employ identical grammatical categories for opposite purposes. Generally, as is the case with prenominal attributes, articles and pronouns, the categories denoting equivalence of the quatrains in *SL 1925* designate contrast in *SL 1892*. The opposite case also holds: possessives, used in the early version as one of the sole means of establishing equivalence between quatrains, are, on the contrary, one of the sole means of contrasting the inner and outer quatrains in the late version.

1925

18.3   Despite the overwhelming preference of the final version for symmetries of equivalence rather than of contrast, the inner quatrain of *SL 1925* differs just as dramatically from the two outer quatrains as does that of *SL 1892*. In consecutive order each line of this quatrain breaks off manifestly from the pattern of the first stanza, which constitutes a separate sentence, detached in the final version from the rest of the text by the only full stop within the poem. As opposed to the outer quatrains, which are built entirely on the principle of coordination, it is based on subordination (see 14.0) and contains the only two verbs of state to be found in the poem (13.5). The initial line of the inner quatrain is the only line in which one finds two finites; moreover, of these, one belongs to the main clause (II $_1$*arose*) and the other —to the first subordinate clause in the text (II $_1$*had*). The second line of this quatrain inaugurates a mirror-image sequence of diversified verbal types echoing the verbs of action, process and state which have appeared so far, but in reverse order. It also opens the set of three similes, which mark the metaphoric constitution of this quatrain as opposed to the metonymic structure of the two outer ones.

18.4   At the border between the two halves of the poem, the third line of the inner quatrain in *SL 1925* opens the distich II $_{3-4}$, the grammatical make-up of which diverges strikingly from all the other lines of the poem. This distich is the only to possess: 1) three personal nouns of the *he*-gender, namely two proper names (II $_3$*Odysseus*, $_4$*Priam*) and the appellative $_4$*peers*; 2) three postpositive semi-predicative attributes (II $_3$*Doomed*, $_4$*proud*, and *murdered*); 3) the only two equational conjunctions ($_3$*like*, $_4$*as*); and 4) the only sociative preposition in *SL 1925* ($_4$*with*). In contradistinction to this distich, the first distich of the same quatrain has three finites (II $_1$*arose*, *had*, $_2$*seemed*) and two nouns of the *she*-gender ($_1$*girl*, $_2$*world* — cf. 6.6). Thus a clear-cut set of features marks the borderline between the two halves of the poem.

18.5   The division of the poem into two halves of six lines each, further subdivided into two triplets, is also suggested by the distribution of certain grammatical categories. In the first half of the poem, three lines devoid of verbs are followed by three lines each containing at least one verb; in the second half, each of the two triplets has a verb in its last line. The definite article also displays a symmetrical distribution by halves and triplets: in the first half, a triplet containing two definite articles per line is followed by a triplet devoid of them; in the second half, a triplet containing one *the* per line alternates with a triplet again devoid of definite articles. Furthermore, the 18 copulative conjunctions and prepositions evenly divide into two sets of 9, one in each half of the poem.

18.60   Another division into two groups of six lines each is clearly suggested by the subject matter. As mentioned above (3.1), in both versions six lines are devoted to the 'overground' and six lines to the 'terrestrial' (*SL 1892*) or 'human' (*SL 1925*) level. This division is supported by the distribution of personal and non-personal nouns and pronouns: the personals are bound exclusively to the six 'terrestrial' or 'human' lines. The two versions differ, however, in the gender characterization of the personal nouns and pronouns of the terrestrial level. In *SL 1892* the four lines of the inner quatrain and the last line of each outer quatrain refer exclusively to the feminine gender. In *SL 1925*, however, the 'human' lines are divided according to gender: those which belong to the second distichs of the quatrains are characterized as masculine (I_4, II_{3-4}, III_4); the others as feminine (II_{1-2}). The grammatical differentiation of the distichs finds consistent expression also in the relative distribution of copulative conjunctions and prepositions (12.1). The division of the quatrains into distichs is furthered by the alternating rhyme scheme (ABAB).

18.61   It is significant that verbs appear in both versions only in the six lines referring to the terrestrial or human level. The only exception to this rule is the bare repetitive transfer from the inner quatrain, III $_1$*Arose*, in *SL 1925* (cf. 15.2).

18.70   The external (marginal) and internal segments of the individual lines are mutually opposed by grammatical means. The line-ends in both versions are delimited by the fact that the rhyme-words are monosyllabic nouns and by the fact that plural nouns are proper in *SL 1925* only, and in *SL 1892* preponderantly, to the rhymes (cf. 6.40 and 6.7).

In *SL 1925* any internal concrete noun enters into a metonymical relation with the following rhyme-word, which in most instances specifies its framework: I ₁*a sparrow in the eaves*, ₂*The *** moon and all the milky sky*; II ₂*A girl *** that had red mournful lips*, ₃*Odysseus and the labouring ships*, ₄*Priam murdered with his peers*; III ₂*A *** moon upon an empty sky*.

18.71   In *SL 1925* the final line of each quatrain is signaled grammatically by the presence of a noun of masculine human gender (I ₄*man's*, II ₄*Priam*, III ₄*man's*) and of a corresponding possessive *his*, referring to these nouns and elsewhere absent, and by the lack of either articles (cf. 11.0) or prenominal attributes (cf. 7.1).

18.72   The transition from one phase to another signaled in *SL 1892* by the pairs of adverbs, II ₁*then* and III ₁*now*, is obliterated in *SL 1925*. There, in agreement with *A Vision* (p. 136), "every image is separate from every other, for if image were linked to image, the soul would awake from its immovable trance". The focus upon time in *SL 1892* and its exclusion in *SL 1925* become particularly palpable when one opposes the six temporal indications of the early version —I ₃*ever- ****, ₄*old*; II ₁*then*, ₄*myriad years*; III ₁*now*, ₄*old* — to the total lack of such indications in the final version.

18.8   In both versions the properties common to the two outer quatrains are evident, whatever their relation (equivalence or contrast) to the inner. The equivalence of the two is semantically underlined, especially in *SL 1925*, where the first three lines in each portray a metonymic contiguity of overground images, visual in the even line, auditory in the odd lines, and thus correspond to the alternation of *man's* visible *image and his* audible *cry* in I₄, III₄. In *SL 1892* the terrestrial level referred to in the last line of each outer quatrain is described solely in auditory images (I₄, III ₄*earth's old and weary cry*).

18.90   The contrariety of the two outer quatrains finds a sharper grammatical expression in the early version, viz. the differences of tense and voice in the verbs through the emergence of the present and passive — III₄ *Are shaken* (cf. 13.4) and the confinement of preposition-less rhyme-words to the first quatrain (cf. 6.43), whereas *SL 1925* has recourse chiefly to lexical means for contrasting the two outer quatrains. For example, an ironical turn inverts the syntactic hierarchy of the first two rhyme-words: in I ₂*sky* is a subject and I ₁*eaves* an adverbial of place, while in the third quatrain the role of subject is assigned to III ₁*eaves*, and ₂*sky* is declassed to an adverbial of place (see further, 19.0 ff. below).

18.91   The compound preterit forms of the predicate in the two outer quatrains of *SL 1925* are semantically opposed to each other: the initial one destructive and turned to the past, the final one constructive and prospective.

SEMANTIC CORRESPONDENCES

19.0   In the epithets of the manuscript version (*SL 1891*) there may be observed what the poet terms "an enforced attraction between Opposites" (*A Vision*, p. 93); III $_3$*The wearisome* [!] *loud chaunting of the leaves* suddenly reappears III $_4$*shaken with earth's old and weary* [!] *cry*.

19.10   In comparison with *SL 1892*, the final version achieves a greater contrast between the two outer quatrains by impoverishing the image of the overground level in the third quatrain, and thus effectively pushes into the foreground the relation between the two opposite spheres. The characters which filled the overground lines of the first quatrain in *SL 1892* and *SL 1925* gradually diminish in number and their epithets become more subdued: I $_1$*a sparrow*, substituted in *SL 1925* for I$_1$ and III $_1$*the sparrows* of *SL 1892*, disappears behind the metonymy III $_1$*clamorous eaves* in the last stanza of the final version; the *famous harmony of leaves* which adorned I$_3$ gives way in III$_3$ to their plain *lamentation*; I $_2$*the star-laden sky* and *the milky sky*, the grammatical subjects of the two versions, change in the final quatrain of *SL 1925* into a mere circumstantial modifier of place with a meager epithet, III $_2$*upon an empty sky*.

19.11   At the end of the two outer quatrains, the possessive *earth's* in *SL 1892* and *man's* in *SL 1925* designate the chief entity of the lower sphere (cf. 3.1). In the early version, I$_2$ and III $_2$*sky* stood in direct opposition to the *earth's* *** *cry* in the next even line of the same quatrains, whereas in the final version an analogous opposition embraces the initial nouns of the equivalent lines I$_2$ and III $_2$*moon* in respect to I$_4$ and III $_4$*man's* (cf. 16.3).

19.20   The threshold of the nineties was for Yeats marked by a "con-

tinual discovery of mystic truths" (*Memoirs*, p. 30); the creation of
SL 1891 belongs to the period of his growing inclination toward esoteric
research, with a faith in the correspondences between the human soul
and body and the planets from Saturn to the Moon (*ibid.*, p. 23).

19.21   The lunar body, as the main symbol in the poet's mythology,
was promoted by Yeats with a particular persistence in the first draft
of his treatise *A Vision* (1925), which was prepared by the poet at the
same time and with as much zeal as the final version of "The Sorrow
of Love" (included by the author in another book of the same year,
his *Early Poems and Stories*). In his note of 1925 to the latter collection
(*Var.*, p. 842) Yeats testifies that he is "now once more in *A Vision* busy
with that thought, the antitheses of day and night and of moon and
of sun"; he immediately turns to the cycle *The Rose* and relates that
"upon reading these poems for the first time for several years" he real-
izes that their heroine has been imagined "as suffering with man and
not as something pursued and seen from afar".

19.22   Already in the early version of *SL* the contrasting images of
I $_2$*The full round moon* and III $_2$*The crumbling* (*1891*:*withered*) *moon*
were apparently related to the author's gradually maturing mystical
doctrine later systematized in *A Vision*. This "philosophy of life and
death" found its poetic embodiment in the *phantasmagoria* "The Phases
of the Moon", first printed in 1919 (*Var.*, p. 821) and later included in
the first edition of *A Vision*. This poem evokes the stage "When the moon's
full" (*Var.*, p. 375, line 75 ff.), immediately followed by "the crumbling of the moon" (*ibid.*, line 87 ff.) and focuses on the diverse effects
of these phases "Upon the body and upon the soul" (*ibid.*, p. 376, line
93). It is significant that from 1895 on, *crumbling* was replaced in *SL*
by the trope *curd-pale*, and that in the final version of the poem these
two telling epithets were supplanted by more remote allusions: I $_2$*The
brilliant moon* and III $_2$*A climbing moon*, the latter ambiguous (climbing toward the zenith or rather toward the next phase?) and the former,
brilliant, according to the author's own acknowledgment, for its "numb-
ness and dullness", so "that all might seem, as it were, remembered
with indifference, except some one vivid image" (*Auto.*, p. 291). That
"one vivid image" must have been the dominant noun *moon* itself, the
central visual motif common to the two pictures of the overground
level in *SL 1925* (cf. 16.3).

19.23   "The full moon is Phase 15", Yeats writes, and "as we approach
Phase 15, personal beauty increases and at Phase 14 and Phase 16 the
greatest human beauty becomes possible" (*Vision*, pp. 78, 131). While

the inner quatrain of *SL* alludes to Phase 15, the two outer quatrains reflect its adjacent Phases.

> Under the frenzy of the fourteenth moon,
> The soul begins to tremble into stillness,
> To die into the labyrinth of itself!
>
> *(Var.*, p. 374, lines 53–55)

"Man's image and his cry", blotted out according to the initial quatrain of *SL 1925*, corresponds to the song of Robartes in "The Phases of the Moon" and to its further lines announcing the full moon:

> All thought becomes an image and the soul
> Becomes a body ***
>
> *(Var.*, p. 374, line 58f.)

— or in the terms of *SL 1925*, II ₁*A girl arose.*

> And after that the crumbling of the moon.
> The soul remembering its loneliness
> Shudders in many cradles; all is changed.
>
> *(Var.*, p. 375, lines 87–89)

As explained in *A Vision* (p. 137f.), "there is always an element of frenzy", but "Phase 16 is in contrast to Phase 14, in spite of their resemblance of extreme subjectivity***. It has found its antithesis, and therefore self-knowledge and self-mastery." Briefly, it is the phase in which all the physical illusions of Phase 14 *Could but compose man's image and his cry.*

19.30   The inner quatrain lacks such pairs of opposites as *sky* and *earth* of *SL 1892* or *moon* and *man* of *SL 1925*. Yet at the same time, the *moon* of the two outer stanzas displays a particular correspondence to the heroine of the adjacent inner quatrain. In *SL 1892* the juxtaposed portrayals of I ₂*The full round moon* and II ₁*those red mournful lips* exhibit a multiple correspondence in the morphological and phonological make-up of the two phrases: *full* — *** *ful* and /r.ndm.n/ — /r.dm.rn/.

19.31   "My love sorrow [!]", says Yeats, "was my obsession, never leaving by day or night" (*Memoirs*, 74), and a passage in the first draft of Yeats' *Autobiography*, with a more than free paraphrase of Leonardo da Vinci's *Notebooks*, throws light on the image of the III ₂*climbing moon* and its counterpart, the "arising" II ₂*girl *** that had red mournful lips* of *SL 1925*: "At last she came to me in I think January of my thirtieth year ***. I could not give her the love that was her beauty's right. *** All our lives long, as da Vinci says, we long, thinking it is but the moon that we long [for], for our destruction, and how, when we meet [it] in the shape of a most fair woman, can we do less than leave all others for her? Do we not seek our dissolution upon her lips?" (*Memoirs*, 88). These lines may be confronted with an earlier paragraph of the same *Memoirs* (p. 72), the poet's confession of his twenty-seventh (3^3) year: "I think my love seemed almost hopeless***. I had never since childhood kissed a woman's lips."

19.32   The outline of Phase 15 in *A Vision* (p. 136) adds that "now contemplation and desire, united into one, inhabit a world where every beloved image has bodily form, and every bodily form is loved. This love knows nothing of desire, for desire implies effort ***. As all effort has ceased, all thought has become image, because no thought could exist if it were not carried to its own extinction."

19.33   The motto to the poet's reflections on the Fifteenth Phase of the Moon reads: "No description except that this is a phase of complete beauty" (*Vision*, p. 135). In *SL 1892* the inner quatrain, centered around this particular phase, strikingly differs from the outer stanzas grammatically and compositionally (cf. 18.10ff.). Each of the two distichs is built on a widely pleonastic scheme. The first two lines display a pun-like juxtaposition of two identical sociative prepositions, one synecdochic (II $_1$*you came with those *** lips*) and the other purely metonymic (II $_2$*with you came the whole of the world's tears*). In *SL 1895* the second distich achieved a heptasyllabic tautology, II $_{3,4}$*And all the trouble of her****, with a salient sound figure, /r.b.l/ — /l.b.r/ (*labouring*) — /r.b.l/.

19.40   The relative isolation of the second stanza with respect to the other quatrains of *SL 1892* is to a certain extent counterbalanced by the equivalent correspondences between the early version of this inner quatrain and a few of the surrounding poems of the cycle entitled *The Rose*. Writing on the birth of "those women who are most touching in their beauty", Yeats states in *A Vision* that Helen was of Phase 14 (p. 132). The reference to Troy, later openly diclosed in *SL 1925*, remains rather obscure in the early version, but is clearly revealed in a poem which neighbors on *SL* in *The Rose* cycle, "The Rose of the World":

> Who dreamed that beauty passes like a dream?
> For *these red lips, with all their mournful pride*,

> *Mournful* that no new wonder may betide,
> *Troy passed away* in one high funeral gleam,
> And Usna's children died.
>
> (*Var.*, p. 111)

19.41   Not only phraseological but also versificational features reveal the affinity between the inner quatrain of *SL 1892* and the other lyrics of the same cycle. The repeated *arose* in II$_1$ and III$_1$ of *SL 1925* prompts one critic, John Unterecker, to see a double vision of "a girl arose" and "a girl, a rose" (1959:159). The line II$_1$ is the only one in the poem with all the first three downbeats followed by a word boundary — *A girl/ arose/ that had/ red**** (cf. in *SL 1892* the corresponding line — II$_1$ *And then/ you came/ with those/ red****, and in *SL 1925* such initial oxytones in the same quatrain as II $_2$*And seemed/*, $_4$*And proud/*); it is interesting to note that the poem "The Rose" (1892) which opens the cycle of the same name (1893, *Var.*, p. 100f.) has the identical rhythm in its first line — "*Red Rose,/ proud Rose,/ sad Rose/ ****", literally repeated at the end of the poem (line 24), as well as in the initial line of the second twelve-line stanza — $_{13}$"*Come near,/ come near,/come near/ *** *".

19.42   We are looking for correspondences between "The Sorrow of Love" and the adjacent poems of *The Rose*, but there is another tempting question, that of key words, abundant in the surrounding verses, which were passed over in silence in *SL*. Together with *SL* the poem "When You Are Old" is addressed to Maud Gonne (cf. Bradford 1961: 454) and is the only other text of *The Rose* cycle composed in three quatrains of iambic pentameter. It is hardly by chance that in this poem, which is placed in the edition of 1892 just before, and in editions from 1895 on immediately after, "The Sorrow of Love", the vocable *love*, confined to the title of *SL*, occurs six times, four times as a verb in the second quatrain (II $_1$*How many loved****, $_2$*And loved your beauty*, $_3$*But one man loved****, $_4$*And loved the sorrows****) and twice as a substantive (II $_2$*with love false or true*, III $_2$**** how Love fled*). In *SL* both love and Helen remain unnamed.

19.5   As to Helen's fate, "is it not because she desires so little, gives so little that men will die and murder in her service?" (*Vision*, p. 133). According to the inner quatrain of *SL 1892*, she is accompanied by *the whole of the world's tears*, while in the ultimate version of this stanza, it is *the world in tears*, the second dramatis persona, which emerges as one of her metaphoric incarnations. Her further embodiments, the men who "die and murder" within the scene of the following distich, complete the list of personal nouns, and their subordinative pyramid pointedly distinguishes the inner stanza of *SL 1925* from the surrounding constructs (cf. 14.1), a dissimilarity further enhanced by the fact that the third central downbeat, which is the heaviest in the two outer quatrains, is the lightest downbeat in the inner stanza (cf. 17.20).

19.6   *The world*, incidentally, is the general character assigned in *A Vision* to the Phases 14, 15, 16 of the Great Wheel, with the subsequent inference *Sorrow* (p.102), and it was under the title "The Sorrow of the World" that *SL 1892 Ind* appeared (cf. 6.8).

19.7   While the similarity association guides the patterning of the inner quatrain of *SL 1925*, in the early version of the poem the leading role belongs to relations of contiguity. The complete lack of human nouns (vs. four in the same stanza of *SL 1925*), the surplus of pronouns (seven vs. two in the final version), and especially the reiterated *you* of *SL 1892*, corresponding to *A girl* of *SL 1925*, all testify to the deictic function which underlies the inner quatrain of the early version. Quantifiers, as II $_2$*the whole of the world's tears* and II $_4$*myriad years*, are akin to the vocabulary of external relationship. The stanza devoted to Phase Fifteen either indicates (*SL 1892*) or names (*SL 1925*), but in either case restrains 'description' (cf. 19.33).

19.8   The critics may argue about which of the two versions is more 'defective' and which of them requires more 'indulgence'. Nevertheless, the exacting selection and arrangement of verbal symbols summoned in "The Sorrow of Love" to build a harmonious system of rich semantic correlations and, in Yeats' own terms, "too much woven into the fabric of [his] work for [him] to give a detailed account of them one by one" (*Var.*, p. 843) indeed warrant the poet's assertion: *And words obey my call.*

REFERENCES

G. D. P. Allt, "Yeats and the Revision of His Early Work", *Hermathena* LXIV (1944), 90–101; LXV (1945), 40–57.

James Bailey, "Linguistic Givens and Their Metrical Realization in a Poem by Yeats", *Language and Style* VIII, No. 1 (Winter, 1975), 21–33.

Yves Bonnefoy (trans.), "Le chagrin de l'amour" *Argile* 1 (Paris 1973), 65.

Curtis Bradford, "Yeats and Maud Gonne", Texas Studies in Language and Literature 3 (1961–62), 452–474.

R. Cowell, *W. B. Yeats* (New York 1969).

Adelyn Dougherty, *A Study of Rhythmic Structure in the Verse of William Bulter Yeats* (The Hague-Paris 1973).

Richard Ellmann, *The Identity of Yeats* (London-New York 1954).

Richard Exner (trans.), "Trübsal der Liebe", in W. B. Yeats, *Werke* I, ed. by W. Vordtriede (Neuwied 1960).

M. A. K. Halliday, "Class in Relation to the Axes of Chain and Choice in Language", *Linguistics* 2 (1963), 5–15.

T. R. Henn, *The Lonely Tower: Studies in the Poetry of W. B. Yeats* (London 1965).

Joseph Hone, *W. B. Yeats* (New York 1943).

Otto Jespersen, *The Philosophy of Grammar* (London 1924).

Paul Kiparsky, "Stress, Syntax, and Meter", *Language* LI, No 3 (Sept. 1975), 576–617.

Louise MacNeice, *The Poetry of W. B. Yeats* (London 1941).

David I. Masson, "Word and Sound in Yeats' 'Byzantium'" *ELH* XX, No. 2, 136–60.

——, "Poetic Sound-Patterning Reconsidered", *Proceedings of the Leeds Philosophical and Literary Society XVI*, Part V (1976), 66–124.

George Monteiro, "Unrecorded Variants in Two Yeats Poems", *Papers of the Bibliographical Society of America* LX, No. 3 (1966), 367f.

T. Parkinson, *W. B. Yeats Self-Critic* (Berkeley-Los Angeles 1951).

S. M. Parrish (comp.), *A Concordance to the Poems of W. B. Yeats* (Cornell, N.Y., 1963).

Marjorie Perloff, *Rhyme and Meaning in the Poetry of Yeats* (The Hague-Paris 1970).

G. B. Saul, *Prolegomena to the Study of Yeats's Poems* (Philadelphia 1957).

Jon Stallworthy, *Between the Lines: Yeats's Poetry in the Making* (Oxford 1963).

R. Stamm, "The Sorrow of Love. A Poem by William Butler Yeats Revised by Himself", *English Studies* XXIX, No. 3 (1948), 79–87.

Barbara Strang, *The Structure of English Grammar* (London 1968).

John Unterecker, *A Reader's Guide to William Butler Yeats* (New York 1959).

Paul Valéry, "Poésie et pensée abstraite", in his *Varieté*, V (Paris 1945).

B. L. Whorf, *Language, Mind, and Reality* (Cambridge, Mass., 1941).

William Butler Yeats, (*Auto.* =) *Autobiography* (New York 1965).

——, *The Countess Kathleen and Various Legends and Lyrics* (London 1892).

——, *Early Poems and Stories* (London 1925).

——, (*Essays* =) *Essays and Introductions* (New York 1968).

——, (*Memoirs* =) *Memoirs: Autobiography — First Draft, Journal*, ed. by D. Donoghue (New York 1973).

——, (*Var.* =) *The Variorum Edition of the Poems*, ed. by P. Allt and R. K. Alspach (New York 1957).

——, (*Vision* =) *A Vision* (London 1925). Our page references are to the revised edition (New York 1956).

V. H. Yngve, "The Depth Hypothesis", *Proceedings of Symposia in Applied Mathematics* XII (1961), 130–38.